Documenting World War II

The Rise of
the Nazis

Neil Tonge

Fellow of the Imperial War Museum, London,
in Holocaust Education

rosen publishing's
**rosen
central**

New York

Published in 2009 by The Rosen Publishing Group Inc.
29 East 21st Street, New York, NY 10010

First Edition

Editor: Camilla Lloyd
Consultants: Dr. R. Gerald Hughes and Dr. James Vaughan
Designer: Phipps Design
Maps: Ian Thompson
Picture researcher: Diana Morris
Indexer and proofreader: Patience Coster

Picture acknowledgments: The author and publisher would like to thank the
following for allowing their pictures to be reproduced in this publication:
Cover photographs: BL and BR: Hulton Archive/Getty Images; AKG Images: 10, 19,
29, 35, 39; Cody Images: 20; Mary Evans Picture Library: 1, 9, 16, 17, 43; Cristel
Gerstenburg/Corbis: 31; Getty Images: 15; Hulton Archive/Getty Images: 7, 28, 38;
Keystone/Getty Images: 12; Popperfoto: 27; Punch Cartoon Library: 33; Slava
Katamidze Collection/Hulton Archive/Getty Images: 44; Staatsgalerie Stuttgart ©
DACS 2007, detail from Grosstadt/Bridgeman Art Library: 25; Topfoto: 5; Ullstein
Bild/AKG Images: 24, 32.

Library of Congress Cataloging-in-Publication Data

Tong, Neil.
  Rise of the Nazis / author, Neil Tong. -- 1st ed.
      p. cm. -- (Documenting World War II)
  Includes index.
  ISBN 978-1-4042-1857-4 (library binding)
  1. Nationalsozialistische Deutsche Arbeiter-Partei--History. 2. National
socialism--History. I. Title.
  DD253.25.T66 2008
  943.086--dc22
                                        2007041462

Manufactured in China

CONTENTS

The German Empire in 1871

The rise of the Nazis can only be explained by looking at the situation in Europe before World War I (WWI). Germany as a single, united country did not exist until after 1871. Until that date, German-speaking people lived in a patchwork of about 30 separate states. Prussia was the largest and most powerful of these. Under the leadership of the Prussian king, the German states were united in 1871, after Prussia had successfully led them in a war against France, then the most powerful country in Europe. The Prussian king became *Kaiser* (Emperor) Wilhelm II of Germany and an industrial superstate was created.

Not all Germans were included in the new state. Austrian Germans, numbering around ten million, joined with Hungary, to head a vast, sprawling empire in central Europe called the Austro-Hungarian Empire. Many previously separate states now in the Empire contained different ethnic groups, such as Czechs, Slovaks, and Serbs. These groups had their own languages and cultures, and wanted some, if not total, independence from the German Empire.

In the new German Empire, power was largely in the hands of the *Kaiser*. The German *Kaiser* appointed the chief government minister, the

chancellor. The *Kaiser* also ruled through a parliament called the *Reichstag*. The members of the

SOURCE

SPEECH

"There is only one person who is master in this Empire and I am not going to tolerate any other."

Kaiser Wilhelm II in a speech in 1891.

Reichstag had considerable powers over taxation and finance. By 1912, the socialists were the largest party in the parliament and were demanding reforms for the working class.

By 1914, the more powerful states of Europe were divided into two opposing alliances. France, fearing an attack from her powerful neighbor, Germany, was a member of the "Triple Entente" (*entente* means a friendly agreement) with Britain and Russia. They agreed to come to one another's aid if they were attacked by Germany. The problem faced by the German commanders was that, if war broke out, they would have to fight Russia and France at the same time on two fronts. The Germans came up with the *Schlieffen Plan* to combat this problem. In this plan, they would defeat France first and then turn to attack Russia, which they believed would be slower in getting its troops ready for war. In any case, the Russians mobilized quickly. Germany was allied to Italy and Austro-Hungary in the "Triple Alliance," but when war broke out, Italy decided to join the Allies instead.

SOURCE

POSTER

This is a cartoon of the *Kaiser* in the 1900s. The *Kaiser* is shown in the bathtub reaching out for Europe, and the caption reads: "*He won't be happy till he gets it.*"

HE WONT BE HAPPY TILL HE GETS IT

EUROPE

The countdown to WWI was swift and began with an assassination. On June 28, Archduke Franz Ferdinand, heir to the Austro-Hungarian throne, and wife, Sophie, arrived in Sarajevo, the capital of Bosnia-Herzegovina, on a royal visit. The couple were killed by a Serb nationalist, who wanted Serbia to break from Austro-Hungary and become independent. When this news reached the capitols of western Europe, it plunged them into war.

Defeat and surrender

Although there were two opposing alliances in Europe, no one expected war to break out in 1914. However, when the Austro-Hungarian Empire's heir to the throne was assassinated, the Empire called on the German people for support against Russian-backed Serbia. Russia, in turn, asked for the support of Britain and France, who came to Russia's aid.

In 1917, after three long years of warfare, Germany was on the edge of defeat. Despite initial advances into France and the defeat of Russia in

1917, Germany's defeat became inevitable when the United States joined the Allies in April of that year. In a last desperate gamble, the Germans launched a series of attacks along the Western Front in the spring of 1918. These offensives failed and as huge numbers of Allied U.S. soldiers arrived, the Germans realized they were doomed. Over a million German soldiers had died in the war and civilians faced starvation as a result of the fighting. Germany did not have the reserves or the will to continue.

An "armistice" (an end to the fighting until peace terms could be

On the eve of World War I in 1919, areas allied to Germany and Germany itself occupied the area in red.

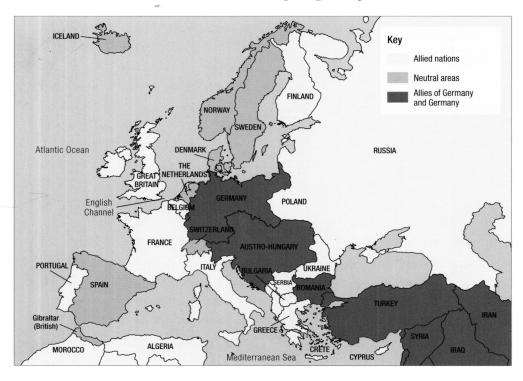

The **Freikorps** *were mainly made up of groups of unemployed ex-soldiers who held extreme nationalist views. This picture shows their armored van with their symbol of the skull and crossbones.*

agreed) was declared on the eleventh hour of the eleventh day of the eleventh month, November 11, 1918, by the commanders of the army: Field Marshal Hindenburg and General Ludendorff. During October and November, a popular revolution swept through Germany, as workers seized control and German sailors mutinied. On November 9, 1918, members of the *Reichstag* declared the formation of a republic. Friedrich Ebert, the leader of the Social Democrats, the largest single party in the *Reichstag*, was elected as chancellor. The *Kaiser* was forced to flee and went into exile.

The new, unstable government was attacked by right- and left-wing political groups. In January 1919, some communists, who took the name *Spartacists*, attempted to overthrow the government. Ebert turned to the bands of extreme nationalist ex-soldiers called the *Freikorps* for help. Berlin was too dangerous for the government to meet in, so they met in the town of Weimar and the Weimar Republic was formed. The *Freikorps* crushed the *Spartacists'* uprising, but Ebert had now put his government into the hands of the military, who had little sympathy for, or loyalty to, the republic. And furthermore, the chancellor had undermined the trust of the working class by putting down a popular rising. The government was still confident that it could make a democratic Germany stable and believed that because of this, it would be treated fairly in the war's aftermath.

The Treaty of Versailles, 1919

The Allies did not have very clear war aims in 1914, but as the war continued, some clearer objectives and motives emerged. U.S. President Woodrow Wilson had outlined "14 points" in January 1918, hoping that they would not only end World War I (WWI), but also be a safeguard against any future wars. He wanted the abolition of secret treaties, freedom of trade between countries, the reduction of weapons, and "self-determination" (whereby different nationalities would have their own government and not be ruled by another power) for all countries. These changes, he believed, would remove the causes of conflict between countries. Germany hoped that these points would form the basis of any peace treaty with the Allies.

Britain and France, however, believed that Wilson's 14 points were too idealistic and would not work. Their two countries had suffered a great deal from the war and they

The map below shows Europe after World War I and the losses for Germany as a result of the Versailles Treaty of 1919.

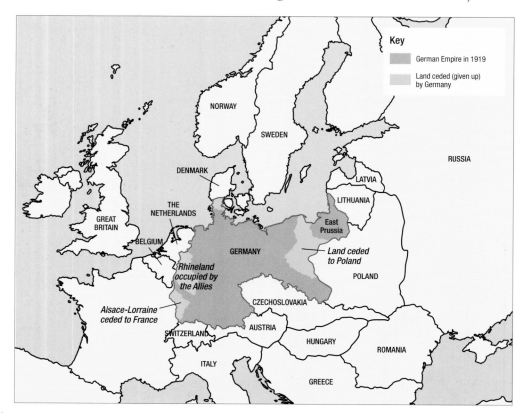

wanted some compensation from Germany for the suffering. In the December 1918 British election campaign, Lloyd George, the British prime minister, had said that Germany would be "*squeezed until the pips squeaked.*" George Clemenceau, the French prime minister, wanted German power permanently reduced so that it would never again be able to threaten France. He wanted German forces to be scaled down, and demanded that part of its territory was taken and given to other countries. Clemenceau agreed that Germany should pay reparations (vast amounts of money) in compensation for the damage caused to France.

In January 1919, the leaders of 32 countries met in Paris to discuss the terms of the treaty. To the surprise and dismay of the German delegates, they were not invited to attend, but were told to await the outcome of the discussions. As the conference proceeded, it became clear that Germany was to be severely weakened as a result of the treaty, so that it would never be capable of waging war again.

When the terms were agreed among the Allies, the treaty was presented to the German delegation. They were deeply shocked at the harshness of the terms. When they refused to sign, they were told that this would result in a continuation of the war. New elections

CARTOON

The Germans saw the punishment of the treaty as the equivalent of the guillotine. The cartoon shows Wilson, Clemenceau, and Lloyd George (the Allied leaders).

Thomas Theodore Heine or Th.Th. Heine in *Simplicissimus* 1919.

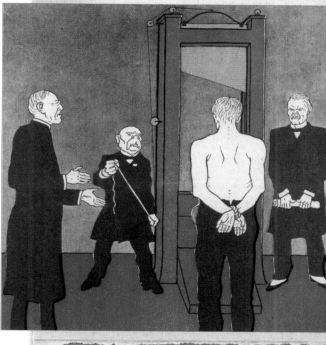

were held in Germany to seek approval from the electorate. The new German government realized that they had no option but to agree to the humiliating terms. Germany reluctantly signed the treaty on June 28, 1919.

Reaction to the treaty

The whole German nation felt the Treaty of Versailles was humiliating and unfair. After 1919, even some Allied politicians began to criticize it as too harsh. Lloyd George suspected that all they had succeeded in doing was building up German resentment, which was sure to cause future conflict. Some historians today feel that the treaty was the worst solution. It was too harsh to be accepted by the German population, yet not harsh enough to stop Germany from becoming powerful again.

However, France felt it was justified. After a costly war, Germany had only lost 13 percent of its prewar territory and 10 percent of its population. As a result of the war, the Austro-Hungarian Empire was broken up into various national countries surrounded by small and unstable states, and was greatly weakened. Despite the reduction in its armed forces, Germany remained potentially powerful. France had only agreed to the terms of the treaty on the condition that Britain and the U.S. would also enter into a defensive alliance. The U.S. Senate and the British government refused to do this.

POSTER

This election poster depicted the government of Jews and socialists as being responsible for the German loss of WWI. Many nationalists believed the government had "*stabbed Germany in the back.*"

From *Der Schlungbrief,* Berlin 1942.

In Germany, the treaty was despised. The German people felt humiliated by their defeat in the war and had thought the treaty might be more lenient because of their new democratic government. The Allies did not allow any room for negotiation and many Germans believed that they had been deceived into seeking an armistice. Nationalists who wanted to see their country strong again argued that the German army had not been defeated but betrayed by the Weimar politicians. The leaders of the German High Command, Field Marshal Hindenburg and General Ludendorff, had resigned when the armistice was declared to avoid being tainted with defeat.

The treaty was signed in November 1918. Nationalists described the politicians who had signed it the "November criminals" who had "*stabbed Germany in the back.*" They attacked the Weimar politicians as "*socialists and Jews,*" who had not protected German honor (see page 10). Although the Weimar politicians had not wanted to sign the treaty, they had not seen an alternative. If they had refused, the Allies would have resumed the war and might have attempted to occupy Germany.

Many disillusioned Germans believed that the army had never lost the war. These nationalists thought they had been betrayed by the November criminals, the Social Democratic Party, who had formed the Weimar Republic. In fact, they were very moderate socialists who had supported the war, and only a few members of the government were Jews.

Although many people in Germany felt that the treaty was far too strict a

SOURCE

NEWSPAPER

"Today in the hall of mirrors [at Versailles] the disgraceful treaty is being signed. Do not forget it! The German people will, with unceasing labor, press forward to reconquer the place among the nations to which they are entitled."

From the German newspaper, *Deutsch Zeitung*, on the day the treaty was signed in 1919.

punishment, it was not as harsh as the Treaty of Brest-Litovsk that Germany had forced Russia to sign in 1917. At this point, Russia had collapsed under a communist revolution and had been forced to ask for surrender terms.

The Treaty of Versailles was severe, but it could have penalized Germany even more. Clemenceau, the French premier, had wanted the Rhineland to become a separate state from Germany, the Saar area to be joined to France, and Danzig to become part of Poland, but these things did not happen.

The early life of Adolf Hitler

Among those people vowing to overthrow the Treaty of Versailles was a corporal in the German army who, in 1919, was in a hospital recovering from a gas attack. His name was Adolf Hitler.

Hitler was born in 1889 near Linz in Austria, where his father was a customs official. At primary school, Adolf became a ringleader in the games he and his schoolmates played. War games were his particular favorite and he was gripped by stories of the Franco-Prussian war. Things changed when he moved to secondary school in 1900. His school reports recorded "*unruly*" behaviour. Hitler wished to become an artist, his father wanted him to be a civil servant. There was much tension

In the trenches, Hitler said he found companionship and purpose that previously had been missing from his life. This picture shows Corporal Adolf Hitler (left, with the cross above his head) with other soldiers in WWI.

between them before Hitler's father died in 1903. When Hitler's mother, whom he adored, died in 1907, he became restless and aimless. He left Linz for Vienna to enter art school but he failed the interview. From 1908 to 1913, he wandered the streets of Vienna, struggling to make a living by painting postcard scenes of the city. He was very poor and lived in hostels. During this time, he picked up many of the anti-Semitic (hatred of Jews) views that were held by many in Vienna. Indeed, Karl Lueger (mayor of Vienna 1897–1910) actively encouraged anti-Semitic demonstrations.

When war broke out in 1914, Hitler immediately went to the Bavarian capital city, Munich, and joined the German army. Despite his Austrian heritage, he hated the multinational Austro-Hungarian Empire. He had gone to Munich before, in 1913, to avoid serving in the Austro-Hungarian army. In August 1914, he received special permission to join the German army. He was a brave soldier and won the Iron Cross twice, first and second class. It was rare for the Iron Cross first class to be awarded to soldiers of the rank of corporal (Hitler's rank) since it was usually reserved for officers. In 1918, Hitler was badly gassed and was in hospital when the armistice was signed. When he heard the terms of the Treaty of Versailles, he was outraged, and in common with other nationalists, blamed Germany's defeat on the communists and the Jews. After the war, Hitler returned to Munich where he began to lecture to groups of soldiers. He gained a reputation as a powerful speaker among the soldiers. He also attended

PARTY PROGRAM

Points from the political program of the German Workers' Party in 1919:

1. We demand the union of all Germans in a Greater Germany.

2. We demand equality of rights for the German people in its dealings with other nations, and the revocation [scrapping] of the Treaty of Versailles.

3. We demand land and territory to feed our people and settle our surplus population.

4. Only members of the nation may be citizens of the state. Only those of German blood, whatever their creed, may be a member of the nation. Accordingly, no Jew may be a member of the nation.

nationalists' meetings. The meeting of a tiny nationalist group, the German Workers' Party, was to prove a turning point in his life.

The Nazi Party 1919–23

When Adolf Hitler became a member of the German Workers' Party, it was tiny, had no money, and not much of a political program. The party, which was founded in January 1919 by Anton Drexler, was an organization of working-class nationalists with only 55 members. Within 14 years, under Hitler's leadership, it had become the most powerful political party in Germany. How did Hitler achieve this success?

Conditions throughout the country allowed nationalist radical groups to form. Germany had been defeated and forced to sign a humiliating peace treaty. There were continuing threats from left-wing revolutionaries and the economic situation was very unstable. It was not only the left-wing groups that threatened the Weimar government in its early days. The army hated the restrictions imposed upon it by the Treaty of Versailles. Many soldiers joined the *Freikorps*. The Allies grew concerned at the growth of unofficial forces within Germany and demanded that they be disbanded. This resulted in the *Kapp Putsch* in 1920, led by Wolfgang Kapp, who marched into Berlin with some *Freikorps* units. The Weimar government was forced to flee to Dresden. The *putsch* collapsed and a general strike resulted.

At first, the German Workers' Party was unknown outside of Bavaria in southern Germany. There were many extreme nationalist groups in existence at the time, all vowing to overthrow the Weimar government and restore Germany to greatness. In early 1919, revolutionaries on the far left had declared Bavaria to be a communist republic. In May 1919, the *Freikorps* and army units had crushed its communist government, killing hundreds of opponents. By 1920, Bavaria was under the control of right-wing nationalists led by Gustav Kahr.

SOURCE

RECOLLECTION

"Leaning from the rostrum as if he was trying to impel his inner self into the minds of all these thousands, he was holding the masses, and me with them, under an hypnotic spell by the sheer force of his beliefs… I forgot everything but the man; then glancing around, I saw that his magnetism was holding these thousands as one."

Kurt Ludecke describing the affect of one of Hitler's speeches on him in the 1920s.

Hitler's brand of nationalistic and racist political views now found fertile ground. Resigning from the army, Hitler entered politics and began to earn a reputation as a brilliant speaker in political rallies in Munich.

The German Workers' Party adopted a new name—the "National Socialist German Workers' Party" (NSDAP, later known as the Nazis) and in 1921, Hitler became its leader. Helped by the Bavarian army with money and recruits, it became the most organized of the right-wing groups. In order to defend the party from attacks and to break up opponents' meetings and impress crowds with its discipline, Hitler created the SA (*Sturm-Abteilung*, or storm troopers). By 1923, Hitler had become a well-known figure in Bavaria.

Hitler played a vital role in the Nazis' success because of his charisma and his powerful speeches. His message was simple and emotional, and appealed to many different people. He spoke of Germany being defeated and weakened by communists and Jews. Remove these enemies, he argued, and Germany would be great again. Hitler had strong principles and he was a superb opportunist who took advantage of any situation that presented itself.

Hitler was a brilliant speaker and delivered very powerful speeches in the early years of the Nazi Party.

The Munich Hall *Putsch*, 1923

By 1919, Germany was in financial chaos as the economy lay in ruins after the war. Those on fixed pensions, for example, the elderly, found it difficult to survive. Workers' wages could not keep up with inflation (the rise in prices). The new Weimar government was wracked by popular uprisings and assassinations.

By 1923, Germany could no longer keep up its reparation payments to France. In response to this, French forces marched into the Ruhr and

Nazis march toward the Munich Beer Hall, where they hoped to declare their overthrow of the Weimar Republic.

occupied the main coal- and steel-producing area of Germany. Many Germans were outraged, and the government called a general strike to halt production and make it impossible for the French to remain. The new German chancellor, Gustav Stresemann, called off the strike and attempted to pay some of the money owed. Stresemann was a committed democrat dedicated to the revision of the Treaty of Versailles, but the right-wing nationalists felt that the Weimar government had proved again that it could not uphold German honor.

Even though Hitler's party was only

3,000 strong and virtually unknown outside of Bavaria, Hitler decided that this moment of crisis was the ideal opportunity to seize power. Many of his followers had reached a fever pitch of excitement, and Hitler wanted to prove he was a man of action. Earlier in 1923, Hitler had organized a "Battle League" of right-wing groups to which General Ludendorff, a hero of WWI, had given his support. The plan was to win control over the right-wing Bavarian government led by Gustav Kahr and then to march on Berlin and overthrow the Weimar government.

On November 8, Kahr was giving a speech at the *Burgerbraukellar* (beer hall) in Munich to leading members of his government. Hitler surrounded the beer hall with his SA men and then, brandishing a revolver, marched in and declared a national revolution. Kahr was taken aback and escaped from the beer hall. He then started to organize his government against the attempted Nazi takeover that Hitler had threatened. When the news reached Berlin, the Weimar government ordered Kahr to crush the armed Nazi uprising.

The following day, Hitler risked all on an armed march through Munich, the capital of Bavaria, believing the people would rise in his support. Instead, Hitler and his followers were met with a hail of bullets and 16 of them were killed. Hitler was pushed, or fell, but managed to escape. Arrested

SOURCE

NEWSPAPER

The front page of a German newspaper *Die Woch* showed Hitler and Ludendorff and described the events of the *Putsch*.

shortly afterward, he was put on trial with General Ludendorff. He used the courtroom as a platform to make passionate speeches. The judges were sympathetic to his cause and although he was sentenced to five years in prison, Hitler served only nine months.

Hitler and the Nazi leadership

By now, Hitler was the undisputed leader of the party. The party elite were fanatical and devoted Nazis, but no other Nazi was equal to Hitler, the *Führer*, or leader. Hitler surrounded himself with like-minded men.

Hermann Goering came from a middle-class family. His father had been the governor of German South West Africa (Namibia). Enlisting in the fledgling German air force in WWI, he earned a reputation as a brave and skilled fighter pilot, shooting down 22 enemy aircraft. An arrogant and self-opinionated man, he could also be witty and charming. He joined the Nazi Party in 1922, and for a while was the leader of the SA. Later, when the Nazis came to power in 1933, he was put in charge of the *Luftwaffe*, the German air force. He was also in charge of preparing the economy for war.

Josef Goebbels was the son of an office worker. He won a place at the University of Heidelberg, where he was awarded a degree in philosophy and literature. Considered unfit to fight in WWI because of a crippled foot, he yearned to play an important part within the Party. His intelligence and political talent were put to good use when he was placed in charge of Nazi propaganda. Goebbels used all available methods to ensure that Nazi ideas were spread to the German people. However, surveys conducted by the SS (*Schutzstaffel*) demonstrated that the propaganda campaigns tended to be more successful with the younger generation than with older people.

Rudolf Hess had been a soldier and a pilot in WWI. He joined the party in 1920 and had huge admiration for Hitler. He became Hitler's private secretary and later, during the war, flew single-handed to Britain, in a vain and mysterious attempt to secure peace.

Heinrich Himmler was an agricultural student before the war; he fought briefly in 1918 when he was old enough to enlist. He saw little action, since the war ended soon after he joined. Frustrated, he joined one of the numerous *Freikorps* bands of ex-soldiers. He joined the party in 1923 and supervised the most brutal aspects of the Nazi regime as head of the SS. He worked hard for the Nazis and was very precise (he even recorded each time he had a haircut and a shave).

Ernst Roehm came from a working-class family, but despite this background became a captain in the German army during WWI. He was brutal and tough, with a violent temper. He joined the *Freikorps* and helped to put down communist uprisings. He headed the SA, the Nazis' private army, but was killed in 1934 (see pages 36–7).

Julius Streicher was born in Bavaria. After WWI, he joined an anti-Semitic organization that merged with the Nazis. Streicher was the publisher of *Der Stürmer* newspaper, part of the Nazi

This picture from the 1930s shows Goering in the middle, Himmler on the right, and Roehm on the left.

propaganda machine. His publishing firm also produced anti-Semitic children's books (see page 39).

Nazi racism

While Adolf Hitler was in prison, he set down his ideas in a book he called *Mein Kampf* (translated as "*My Struggle*" or "*My Battle*"). In the book, he describes life as a brutal struggle for survival in which only the strongest nations, races and individuals survived. He believed that Germany deserved to be the greatest nation in the world, because

Hitler is shown on the right of the picture posing in prison with his fellow inmates in 1924. His stay there was comfortable and he was allowed to see visitors.

its people were the "master race." All other races, he wrote, were inferior and the greatest threat to the German race was the Jews. Hitler held the Jews responsible for all the ills of the world, believing that, because they lived in many countries, they were plotting to take control of the world. They would bring about world domination with the help of rich Jewish bankers and financiers, or through the communist revolution that had begun in Russia.

Some leading bankers and leaders of the communist revolution were Jews, and this led some to believe Hitler's claims.

Hitler insisted that the German people must remain racially superior and that this could be achieved by forbidding marriage between races. The Nazis called the Germans the *volk,* or the Aryan race, and they believed that as the race expanded, they would need more living space for their increased population. To achieve this, German forces would need to fight for *lebensraum,* or living space, in Eastern Europe, and those inferior races they conquered would then be enslaved to work for them.

To achieve the purity of the Aryan race, all those considered "*not worthy of life*"—the mentally and physically disabled, for example, were to be "*removed.*" When the Nazis came to power they passed a law allowing the forced sterilization (a medical operation to prevent the birth of babies) of those with mental illnesses. By 1939, this program had developed into one of mass murder, as disabled and mentally ill children were killed by injection or by gas. The Nazis then targeted adults with disabilities. By 1944, over 200,000 people had been murdered in this way.

The Nazis did everything in their power to encourage healthy Germans to have children and increase the Aryan population. Mothers who had

BOOK

"There must be no more majority decision. The decision shall be made by one man, only he alone may possess the authority and the right to command.

"Blood mixture and the resultant drop in the racial level is the sole cause of the dying out of the old cultures. All who are not of good race are chaff [the husk of the wheat that is thrown away as useless for flour]. In Russian Bolshevism [Communism], we must see the attempt undertaken by the Jews to achieve world domination."

Adolf Hitler: extracts from *Mein Kampf,* published in 1925.

large families were given an award— the Mother's Cross: gold for those with eight children, silver for those with six.

After 1933, doctors and scientists offered classes on race and school children were given lessons where they were taught about Aryan superiority. All other groups considered to be outside of the *volk,* such as beggars, gypsies, homosexuals, alcoholics, and repeat criminal offenders, were shunned and eventually sent to concentration camps. Jews, however, remained Hitler's main object of hatred.

The Nazis change their tactics

In December 1924, Hitler was released from prison to find an improved political situation for the Weimar government. The new republic had faced major political and economic problems, but it had survived them. This was because the extremist groups of the right and left had failed to attract mass support and really threaten the government. Although the army was not committed to democracy, it also did not want to see the chaos that would occur in Germany if the republic was overthrown.

LETTER

"When I pursue active work, it will be necessary to achieve a new policy. Instead of working to achieve power by an armed coup, we will have to hold our noses and enter the Reichstag *against Catholic and Marxist members. If outvoting them takes longer than outshooting them, at least the result will be guaranteed by their own Constitution. Sooner or later we shall have a majority, and after that—Germany."*

Hitler in a letter from prison, 1923.

It looked as though the worst was over and the Weimar government could start to establish firm roots. President Ebert had taken firm action to restore order and Chancellor Stresemann had managed to control inflation.

Gustav Stresemann was born in Berlin and won a place at a university, where he distinguished himself. He joined the "German People's Party (DVP)" and was elected to the *Reichstag* in 1907. He came to believe that the situation in Germany could only be improved by the means offered by the Weimar Republic. As chancellor, he helped to strengthen the currency, and other European countries became more optimistic about the democratic future of Germany with him in charge.

Hitler had several tasks to accomplish. He needed to rebuild his party and secure his leadership. Also, much to his distaste, he had become convinced that the party would have to use the democratic process to get into power, through taking part in elections and gaining seats in the *Reichstag*.

While Hitler had been in prison, the Nazi Party had been banned and had been forced to continue its activities as an underground movement. The party had started to fall apart as different, opposing factions formed. In 1926, however, Hitler called a party conference at Bamberg in southern

Germany. He had no intention of allowing anyone else to decide matters and spoke for five hours to the conference, interrupted only by huge rounds of applause. By mid-1926, he was firmly in charge again, but Party membership had fallen to 35,000. The SA (see page 15) was still difficult to control and the comparable paramilitaries of the communists were a stronger force. At this time, Hitler set

PARTY STATISTICS

This graph shows the increase in Nazi Party membership from 1925 to 1929.

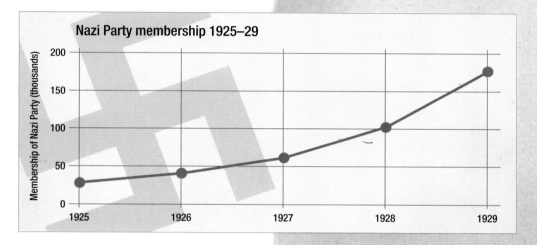

Nazi Party membership 1925–29

up a special force—the SS—as his own personal bodyguard. This organization was to play a major role in ensuring Nazi rule over Germany when the Nazis came to power.

Hitler also set about reorganizing the party. Germany was divided into regions, each of which had a *Gauleiter* (leader). These regions were divided into districts under the control of *Kreisleiters*. Towns and cities had their own Nazi organizations and officials, and Nazi units were evident in every level of society. The SA was brought

under control of Franz von Salomon, an ex-*Freikorps* member and *Gauleiter* of Upper Bavaria. Children were urged to join the "Hitler Youth" to encourage young allegiance to the party. Hitler realized that he needed to increase party membership throughout Germany. As a result, he concentrated on diverse issues that were popular in different parts of Germany. However, although the republic and economy were becoming more stable, the Nazis could not hope to win mass support.

Hope and recovery 1924–8

Despite Nazi claims that the republic was corrupt and that it was failing to improve the lives of the German people, the years following Hitler's release from prison were ones of hope and recovery for the Weimar Republic. Although Stresemann had resigned as chancellor in November 1923, he was the driving force behind the republic's recovery. As foreign secretary from 1923 until 1929, Stresemann had two objectives. Firstly, to revise the crippling reparation payments so that the economy would improve, and secondly, to re-establish a respectable position for Germany within Europe.

Under the "Dawes Plan" 1924 (Charles G. Dawes was a U.S. financier who acted as chairman of the committee that met to discuss Germany's reparations), Germany received a massive loan from the U.S. to kick-start her industries, and the reparations Germany had to pay were initially reduced to lessen the burden. The Nazis attacked the Plan as "*a second Versailles,*" because it gave the U.S. power over the German economy. The Dawes Plan ran until 1928 when there was another conference in 1929, led by Owen D. Young (head of General Electric Company, a U.S. firm), which was attended by an Allied committee. The decision of the committee was that Germany was to continue paying

POSTER

This anti-Semitic Nazi election poster from 1924 depicts a Jewish figure holding the German nation in the chains of the Dawes Plan. The words of the poster are "*Down with financial slavery! Vote National Socialist.*"

Hans Schweitzer, 1924 (Archiv Gerstenberg).

reparations for 59 years and would finish doing so in 1988. Hitler wasted no time in publically denouncing the Plan. It was not only the Nazis who objected to the Plan; many Germans felt that they were being punished for a war that had not been solely their responsibility. However, after much arguing, the *Reichstag* finally agreed to the terms.

Stresemann, now foreign minister, realized that a new relationship with France was crucial if Germany was to be accepted again among the European nations. In 1925, he succeeded in getting French and Belgian troops withdrawn from the Ruhr region of Germany. They had been stationed there to ensure that Germany paid its reparations.

In 1925, a conference was called at Locarno in Switzerland for the countries of western, central, and Eastern Europe to discuss the cause of international conflict. At the conference, Stresemann stated that Germany had agreed the borders with France and Belgium and that no German troops should be stationed in the Rhineland. However, he refused to accept the frontiers with Poland and Czechoslovakia, although he stated that Germany would never use force to change them. Stresemann had succeeded in reaching an agreement with the major European powers without surrendering anything.

PAINTING

This painting by the popular German artist, Otto Dix, illustrates the high life and corruption that the Nazis claimed were the hallmarks of the republic.

In 1926, Germany joined the League of Nations. The League had been set up after WWI to settle international disputes. However, by 1929, Stresemann had become worn out with work and with fending off attacks from the right wing. In October 1929, Stresemann died suddenly from a heart attack at the age of 51.

The Great Depression, 1929

Stresemann died at the point at which the Weimar Republic faced its most severe test. In October 1929, disaster struck the New York stock exchange on Wall Street. Stocks had risen well above their real value. As this dawned on investors, they began to sell in panic. Prices of shares fell rapidly as U.S. investors rushed to sell their shares. On October 30, the New York stock market collapsed totally. Faced with falling investment, production slowed and many factories were forced to close. Millions of U.S. citizens became unemployed.

As the world began to slide into depression, U.S. banks recalled their loans from around the world. In 1927 and 1928, the German government borrowed five times the amount it needed to pay the reparations bill. German businesses were forced into bankruptcy, because they could not meet the loan repayments they had made to survive. By 1932, at least six million, four out of every ten people, were unemployed. Millions of others had to accept low wages or only part-time work. The slow recovery that had begun to take place in farming was thrown into reverse. From 1930 onward, the government, led by Heinrich Brüning, raised taxes and cut state benefits and wages. Millions were now in dire poverty.

It seems likely that Hitler and the Nazis would have remained on the fringes of German politics had it not been for the catastrophe of 1929. In the national elections in 1928, the Nazis secured only 2.8 percent of the vote. However, the depression had a powerful effect on the Weimar Republic. Many Germans believed that democracy had failed them. Between 1930 and 1932, there were five national elections, as a succession of governments tried to make alliances with other political parties to rule Germany. Increasingly, Hindenburg, who had been elected as president in 1925, relied on presidential decrees (making laws without consulting the *Reichstag*) to pass laws to ensure that Germany was governed effectively. By September 1930, a large number of antidemocratic deputies had been elected, especially from among the Nazis. This trend continued into 1932.

As the depression worsened, Nazi representatives increased—from 12 deputies in 1928, to 107 in 1930 and 288 in 1932. Communist deputies to the *Reichstag* also increased from 54 in 1928 to 81 in 1933. The middle ground of politics began to fall away, with the Social Democrats Party and the Democratic Party losing deputies. The German electorate was shifting toward the extremes, particularly toward the right-wing groups, in an attempt to find solutions to the economic depression.

Hitler's appeal and the strength of the Nazi Party grew accordingly. While the Weimar Republic offered only short-term solutions, Hitler's strong and decisive leadership had become more and more attractive to voters.

industrial or urban areas; and in northern Germany and Protestant places rather than in southern Germany and Catholic places. They always adjusted their policies to win

During the Great Depression, soup kitchens were set up to provide for the unemployed. The government also kept food prices high to protect the farmers. As a result, many unemployed people could not afford to eat.

Like any other political party, the Nazis were more successful in some areas than others and attracted a variety of different supporters. In general, they were more successful in middle-class areas than in working-class areas; in rural regions rather than

votes and were most successful when they emphasized their anticommunist beliefs and promised to solve unemployment. Anti-Semitism was sometimes played down and the middle-class became the main focus of their campaign.

27

Nazi tactics

Hitler was central to the success of the Nazi Party. He had won fame initially by his bold defense at his trial in 1923. He had been able to formulate his political ideas in his book, *Mein Kampf,*

organization. For example, the Nazi Welfare Organization formed soup kitchens and handed out food packages to the needy. They paid great attention to local issues and held face-

POSTER

This Nazi election poster says *"We are building!"*. It proclaims that the building blocks of the Nazi agenda are *"Bread, Freedom, and Work"* and contrasts this with the *"lies, smears, unemployment, social degradation, corruption, terror, and a reduction of services"* of their rivals.

NSDAP poster, 1933.

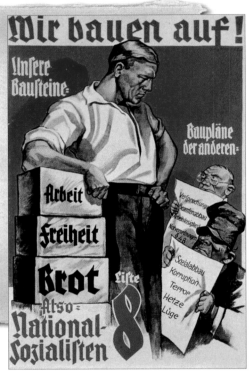

and had restored order from the chaos into which the Nazi Party had fallen while he had been in prison. Hitler possessed a huge amount of willpower that gave people faith in him. In contrast, other political parties seemed to have little sense of direction. He was a powerful speaker who could whip the audience into a frenzy of excitement.

The Nazi Party's success also stemmed from its effective

to-face meetings in local areas. The party also used posters to convey simple messages in a dramatic form.

The Nazi public speakers were required to attend a training school and be licensed. The party used all available means of technology, such as slide shows and movies, to convey their political message. They promised to create an Aryan community that would look after the needs of the German *volk*. They also said that economic problems would be solved and that every German would be provided with bread and work. This would be achieved, they argued, by ending the corrupt rule of the Weimar Republic and replacing it with strong leadership. Communism would be crushed, the Versailles Treaty torn-up, reparations ended, and above all, the Jewish influence over German society would be removed.

The SA played a major role in the Nazi success. Despite the violence they caused, they gave the impression that they were challenging and combating communism. Many people wanted this. Their disciplined marches persuaded many that the Nazis would provide a firm government.

In 1932, Hitler entered the presidential elections against Hindenburg. There were two rounds in the elections. The two candidates to receive the most votes in the first round would go through to a second round. In the first round, Hindenburg won 49.6 percent of the vote, almost an outright majority. Hitler came second with a remarkable 30.1 percent. In the second round, Hitler did slightly better

with 36.7 percent of the vote, but Hindenburg still won easily. Hitler then set his sights on becoming chancellor. To achieve this, he would need President Hindenburg's help, for the president decided who to appoint as chancellor.

Paul von Hindenburg had a military background. He had been a general in WWI and had won stunning victories over the Russians in 1914 and 1915. He was transferred from the Eastern Front to the Western Front and became chief of staff of the army. Along with General Ludendorff, he formed what was virtually a military dictatorship in Germany until 1918. In 1925, Hindenburg replaced Ebert as president and remained in that post until his death in 1934.

SOURCE

POSTER

This Nazi election poster of 1932 proclaims Hitler to be the *"last hope"* for the German people. In the darkest days of the depression, Hitler is presented as the *Führer*, the leader, who alone can restore Germany to greatness.

NSDAP poster, 1932.

Hitler becomes chancellor in January 1933

In spite of their success in the elections of 1932, the Nazis did not have an overall majority. However, as leader of the largest single party, Hitler expected to be invited by the president to become chancellor. However, Hindenburg thought Hitler was too extreme for this important job and instead offered him the position of vice chancellor under a conservative politician, Franz von Papen. Hitler thought this job was beneath him and turned the offer down in anger. The leader of the SA, Roehm, suggested that they should seize power illegally, but Hitler was not sure if the army would back him and at this point refused. Franz von Papen was not a popular politician. He had attained his positions of power through his connections with the aristocracy, with industrialists, and in particular, with Hindenburg.

Franz von Papen had little support in the *Reichstag*. The Nazis, Social Democrats, Communists, and the Center Party were not part of his government. The Nazis and the Center Party raised a vote of "no confidence" in von Papen and won decisively by 512 votes to 42. New elections were called: Hitler and the Nazis threw themselves into the campaign with energy and enthusiasm. Their election posters showed strong, German Nazis and criticized the "weak" government led by von Papen.

The results were disappointing for the Nazis, who lost 34 seats, but they still remained the largest single party, with 196 seats and 33 percent of the vote. Hindenburg had no choice but to offer the post of chancellor to Hitler, but refused him the right to rule by presidential decree (the right to pass laws without consulting the parliament). Hitler turned the offer down once again. The president was in a difficult position. He could not reappoint von Papen, who was his first choice, because von Papen had very little support in the *Reichstag*. Instead, Hindenburg invited another conservative politician, Kurt von Schliecher, to become chancellor. Schliecher also had minimal support in the *Reichstag* and suggested to the president that they set up a military dictatorship instead. Hindenburg refused.

Franz von Papen believed that he could control Hitler if he could get back into a position of power. He made a secret visit to Hitler in Cologne and agreed to back him. Returning to Berlin, von Papen persuaded Hindenburg to accept Hitler as the new chancellor. He calmed Hindenburg's fears by telling him that the conservative forces in the new government would restrain itler's actions. The near-senile 85-year-old Hindenburg finally agreed to the proposal and summoned Hitler to a meeting. On the morning of January 30, 1933, Adolf Hitler became chancellor of Germany.

Hitler's appointment effectively meant the end of the republic.

The Great Depression had had a major effect on its collapse. It added to fears that the democratic system was too weak to offer a solution to the economic disaster. The increase in the number of antidemocratic deputies in the *Reichstag* meant that by 1932, it had become almost impossible for any government to gain its support. Faith in the system of parliamentary government collapsed, leaving a situation that Hitler was able to exploit to the full.

SOURCE

POSTER

This poster with the words: "*Enough now! Elect Hitler!*" is a typical example of the Nazi election posters of 1932. It shows the Nazis breaking out of the chains created by von Papen and the *Reichstag*.

NSDAP poster, 1932.

The *Reichstag* fire, February 1933

The Nazis were jubilant. Their leader had now been appointed to the most powerful political position in Germany. They celebrated with a torchlight procession through Berlin. But Hitler's hold on power was fragile, for there were only two other Nazis in the cabinet: Wilhelm Frich, minister of the interior and Hermann Goering, minister for Prussia. Nationalists and Catholics outnumbered the Nazis. Franz von Papen, as vice chancellor, believed that he could control Hitler.

Hitler immediately set about making his hold over the government more secure. He called for new elections to take place on March 5, and was determined to use his position to secure as many votes as possible. The Nazis were well-funded and spent a great deal of money on the campaign. They also used violence and intimidation to secure votes. Hermann Goering controlled the police and the civil service. He ensured that anyone opposed to the National Socialists were thrown out of their jobs and replaced with Nazis. Fifty thousand extra policemen were recruited under the

This triumphant torchlight procession in Berlin took place as Hitler became chancellor in January 1933.

command of the SA and SS.

As the election campaign neared its climax, an event occurred that greatly benefited the Nazis. On February 27, the *Reichstag* building mysteriously caught fire and was burned to the ground. A Dutch communist, van der Lubbe, was found inside the building. Whether he acted alone or on orders from others is not known, since the court established only his personal guilt. He was sentenced to death and executed. The communists, in fact, had nothing to gain from the fire, because they knew such action would result in imprisonment. Others at the time and since have claimed that the Nazi leadership was involved in starting the fire, for such an act of vandalism would justify a government crackdown and freer use of the emergency decree.

The Nazis immediately claimed that they had uncovered a communist plot to seize the government. When he heard news of the fire, Goering is reported to have said to a British journalist: "*This is a God-given signal. If this fire, as I believe, turns out to be the handiwork of the Communists, there is nothing that will stop us from crushing out the murderous pest with an iron fist.*"

With the use of the emergency powers, Hitler gave the order for his political enemies to be rounded up and thrown into prison. Hermann Goering gave the order for 4,000 Communist Party leaders to be arrested because of their alleged

CARTOON

This cartoon from the British *Punch* magazine shows Hitler being carried on the shoulders of von Papen and Hindenburg in a "temporary triangle" of power with Hitler at the top.

Punch cartoon, 1933.

THE TEMPORARY TRIANGLE.

involvement in the fire. Hindenburg then signed an Emergency Decree for the Protection of the German People, which suspended democratic rights and became the legal basis for Hitler's dictatorship.

The Enabling Act

The result of the elections had given the Nazi Party 288 seats in the *Reichstag*, but had still not produced an overall majority. (There were 647 seats in the *Reichstag*, so the National Socialists fell short of a majority by 40 seats.) Hitler still needed the support of other parties.

On March 21, Goebbels organized a ceremony at the Potsdam Garrison Church to mark the opening of the newly elected *Reichstag*. He invited President Hindenburg, the son of the exiled *Kaiser* and leading army generals to show that Hitler could be trusted in the company of leading figures in Germany. Wreaths were laid on the graves of Prussian kings and Hitler made a deep bow as he shook Hindenburg's hand.

Two days later, the new deputies of the *Reichstag* met at the Kroll Opera House in Berlin. Hitler wanted to change the Constitution to give himself absolute power. To do so, he needed the agreement of two-thirds of the deputies. Only the nationalists, with their 52 seats, agreed to support him. How was he to get the extra votes he needed? The other parties could still out-vote him. The 81 Communist Party deputies had already been banned from the *Reichstag* and many of the Social Democrats were missing either out of fear, or because they were injured following SA violence. Some had fled the country.

The SS surrounded the opera house. Inside SA troops stood glowering at and menacing the non-Nazi deputies. Hitler wanted to be given complete decision-making powers for four years without having to refer to the *Reichstag*. He wanted to achieve this through the passing of an "Enabling Act," which would allow the chancellor and not the president to draft new laws and make treaties with other states.

When Hitler first spoke, he was calm and moderate. He said: "*The government intends to make use of this Act only to the extent required to carry out vitally necessary measures. The existence of the* Reichstag *is not threatened.*" Hitler

RECOLLECTION

"We tried to dam the flood of Hitler's accusations with interruptions ... But that did us no good. The SA and SS people hissed loudly and murmured 'Shut-up!', 'Traitors!', and 'You'll be strung up today!'"

A Social Democrat member of the *Reichstag* describing the passing of the Enabling Act in March 1933.

Hitler greets Hindenburg at the opening of the Reichstag in Potsdam in 1933.

finished his speech and sat down to thunderous applause and then his deputies broke into the German national anthem, "*Deutschland Uber Alles.*"

It took a brave man to stand up and oppose the bill. Otto Wels, the leader of the Social Democrats, got to his feet and made a defiant speech. Hitler flew into a rage. "*I do not want your votes,*" Hitler screamed, "*your death knell has sounded.*"

There were no further speeches. Hitler got his wish. The Enabling Act was passed by 441 votes to 94, with the Social Democrats opposing it. Hitler had now rid himself of the *Reichstag* and the conservative nationalists who believed they could control him.

Even Hitler's old ally, General Ludendorff, who had since fallen foul of Hitler, declared to Hindenburg, "*This damnable man will plunge our Reich into the abyss and bring inconceivable misery down upon our nation.*"

The Night of the Long Knives, June 30, 1934

Hitler then turned his attention to removing any possible opposition to his rule within Germany. All elections were abolished. On May 2, trade union offices were occupied and funds were seized. The unions were replaced by the Nazi German Labor Front.

Within two years of taking power, the Nazi Party had brought almost all organizations within Germany under its control. The political parties that remained disbanded themselves because of Nazi intimidation, and no other political parties were allowed.

While opposition outside the party crumbled away, there were some within the party who wanted National Socialism to move further toward socialism. Some SA leaders and other members of the party were more associated with socialism than nationalism; many of these men wanted to replace the old ruling elite with leading Nazis. This group was viewed as a threat by the more conservative army leaders and the businesses that had supported Hitler's rise to power. Ernst Roehm, leader of the SA, was a prominent member of this more socialist group. He continually criticized the Nazi leadership, and warned the SA and SS against "*false friends*" and "*going to sleep*

or being betrayed at the halfway stage by noncombatants." In a newspaper article, he even described Hitler as "*rotten.*"

Roehm wanted the army absorbed into the SA. The officer class was horrified and looked to Hitler to prevent this from happening. At first, Hitler tried to reason with Roehm, but he had secretly decided that all rivals within the party were to be killed. These rivals were also to include any conservative members of the party who were thought of as dissenters. During the night of June 29 and into the morning of June 30, Hitler flew to Munich where Roehm and the SA were at a Nazi rally. Roehm was arrested, and after he refused to shoot himself, was executed two days later. Other SA leaders linked to him were arrested on their way to the meeting and later executed. Goering ordered the arrests of others throughout the country. It is estimated that 77 leading Nazis and about 100 others within the party were killed on the night of June 29, later the massacre became known as "the Night of the Long Knives."

Hitler also took the opportunity to rid himself of other opponents outside the party. Two army generals, some members of the Catholic clergy, and Gustav Kahr, the man who had betrayed him in the Munich Hall *Putsch*, were also executed. The SA lost its importance within the party and from this moment on, the SS, a smaller, more highly disciplined force, took over. The *Reichstag*, which was now little more than a Nazi assembly, declared Hitler's actions to be entirely legal.

On August 2, 1934, President Hindenburg died at the age of 87. He had been president for nine years. Within hours of his death, Hitler declared that the positions of chancellor and president would be merged. His new title would be *Führer* (leader) or *Reichskanzler* (the president and chancellor). With these powers, he was now commander in chief of the armed forces as well.

Historians agree that Hitler dominated Germany from 1933 until 1945, but they do not always agree on how he used his power. Hitler believed he was acting in the interests of, and according to the will of, the *volk*. After the Enabling Act, he could make laws without involving the *Reichstag* at all. Even ideas that occured to him in his conversations with other Nazi leaders became laws when he told officials to put them into practice.

Hitler's main agency of control was the SS. Until 1933, each state had had its own police force. After 1936, they were all placed under the command of Heinrich Himmler. The SA was disarmed and most of its power was taken away, although it was still used for intimidation. The SS had originally been used as Hitler's personal bodyguard. In 1929, it numbered only 129 but by 1939, it had over 240,000 members. The SS could arrest anyone it chose, and between 1933 and 1939, 225,000 Germans were found guilty of political crimes and were imprisoned as a result. The SS was organized into army fighting units known as the *Waffen-SS*. The "Death's Head" or "Skull" units, or SS-TV (*SS-*

OATH

"I swear by God this sacred oath: that I will render unconditional obedience to the Führer of the German Reich and people, Adolf Hitler, the Supreme Commander of the Armed Forces, and will be ready as a brave soldier to risk my life at any time for this oath."

The army's personal oath of loyalty to Hitler as the *Führer* in 1934.

Totenkopfverbände) were part of the *Waffen-SS* that would later run the concentration camps. At the Nuremburg Trials (1945–9), the SS was declared to be a criminal organization, and many of its members were found guilty of war crimes and crimes against humanity.

Making a racial state

According to Nazi beliefs, the Aryan race needed to be purified by the elimination of all elements of other races and the physically and mentally disabled from society. In 1933, the practice of compulsory sterilization was made legal. Over 400,000 names were submitted to health courts, which made the decision as to who would be sterilized and in over 80 percent of the cases, the sterilization was carried out.

Around 48,000 boys and 5,000 girls attended the Nazi Party Congress rally in Nuremberg and cheered and saluted Hitler's speech.

In 1933, there were about 500,000 Jews living in Germany, less than one percent of the population. Hitler had deeply held, anti-Semitic views and had always identified the Jews as the particular cause of Germany's misfortunes. In March 1933, Nazi mobs beat up many Jewish people and destroyed their property. From April 1933 onward, the Jews were banned from a host of professions, such as medicine, education, and the law. By making life difficult for Jews, the Nazis hoped that they would emigrate to escape persecution. In 1933, 37,000 left Germany, including some very famous people, such as the scientist Albert Einstein. However, Jews who emigrated were in danger of having their property confiscated and they were not allowed to take money out of the country. Other countries in Europe were reluctant to accept the Jews, because they were afraid that the added pressure of more people would lead to to an increase in domestic unemployment.

Hitler used the occasion of the massive party rally at Nuremburg in September 1935 to step up the persecution of the Jews and to announce sweeping measures against them. Introducing the new laws, Hitler declared that he hoped they would provide a future basis for German-Jewish relations, but if this failed then he would have to seek a "Final Solution." These Nuremburg Laws announced that Jews were "aliens" and were no longer to be seen as German citizens.

In 1936, Germany staged the Olympic Games and Hitler called a halt to many of the more obvious acts of anti-Semitism, afraid that some countries might withdraw in protest.

ILLUSTRATION

This is a Nazi children's cartoon with the anti-Semitic words *"The Devil is the Father of all Jews."*

Book illustration by E. Bauer published by Stürmer Press in 1936.

However, in 1937, the campaign against the Jews was renewed. Goering issued an order closing down a wide variety of Jewish businesses. In November 1938, a pogrom against the Jews called *Kristallnacht* (Night of Broken Glass) occured, when Jewish shops and homes were ransacked and many Jews were beaten to death. This violence spread as Germany annexed Austria the same year. The Nazis looted the homes of 200,000 Austrian Jews.

In August 1938, Adolf Eichmann set up a Central Office for Jewish Emigration in Austria. Himmler's right-hand man, Reinhard Heydrich, set up an equivalent office in Germany. By November 1938, 50,000 Jews had left Austria and 150,000 Jews had emigrated from Germany.

There were other victims of the Nazi persecution, too. They included gypsies, homosexuals, Jehovah's Witnesses, and Black people.

The road to war

While Hitler was consolidating his power in Germany, he was also preparing for a war he thought was inevitable. He believed that there was a need to unite all German-speaking people into one country and to conquer land in the east as *lebensraum* for the German people (see page 21). On March 3, 1936, Hitler sent troops into the Rhineland. This area was meant to remain demilitarized under the terms of the Treaty of Versailles, so this was a direct challenge to France. Consequently, France called on Britain for support, but the British did not want to enter into a war and were not prepared to act at this point. Hitler's success attracted Benito Mussolini, the dictator of Italy, to make an alliance between the two states. Italy and Germany formed what they called the "Axis" partnership. Soon afterward, Japan signed an Anti-Comintern Pact with Italy and Germany, aimed at defending themselves collectively against the spread of communism from the Soviet Union. In the pact, all three nations agreed to enter the war if the Soviet Union became involved.

Two years later, Hitler challenged the terms of the Treaty of Versailles still further. The treaty had forbidden the union of Germany and Austria, even though many of the inhabitants of Austria were German-speaking. Hitler summoned Schuschnigg, the chancellor of Austria to a meeting and ordered him to appoint Austrian Nazis to his government. Schuschnigg quickly realized that this was the start of an attempted takeover of Austria. The Austrian chancellor ordered a vote to see if the Austrians really wanted union with Germany. The German Nazis did not want to run the risk of the vote going against them, and so, claiming that law and order had broken down, they sent German troops into Austria. There was no resistance, and under a vote supervised by the Nazis, 99 percent of Austrians voted for the union, or *Anschluss.* Again, Britain and France were not prepared to oppose Hitler's move, since neither country wanted to embark on another war and the people of Austria appeared to have voted for *Anschluss* in overwhelming numbers.

Czechoslovakia was Hitler's next target. The country had been created in 1918 out of part of the Austro-Hungarian Empire. It was inhabited mainly by Slavs, although there was a population of three million German-speaking people in the Sudetenland, which bordered Germany and Austria. Hitler demanded that this land be joined to the Third Reich.

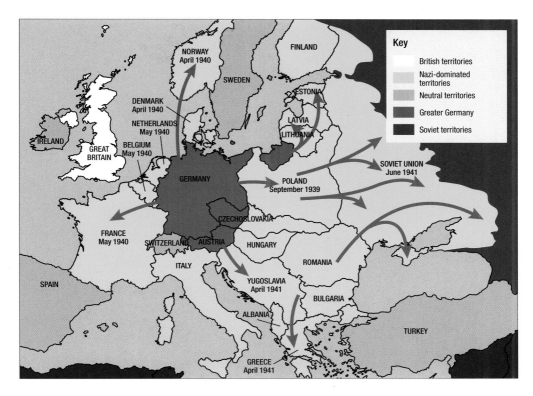

The Czechs hoped that they could rely on Britain and France to come to their aid, but instead, the two powers allowed Hitler to occupy the Sudetenland. Giving in to Hitler's demands in this way became known as "appeasement." By March 1937, German forces had occupied all of Czechoslovakia. Hitler assured Britain and France that he had no more territorial demands to make, but this time neither country was convinced and they began to arm for war.

Hitler then demanded land in the German-speaking parts of Poland. This time Britain and France were more resolute in their opposition to Nazi Germany's expansion in

The map above shows Nazi land gains in Europe. By May 1940, Hitler had dominated much of Europe from France to Poland and from Norway to Greece.

Europe. Hitler chose to ignore Britain and France.

On September 1, 1939, German soldiers in Polish uniforms faked an attack on a German radio station and the German invasion of Poland began. After warning Germany that it must withdraw its troops from Poland, Britain and France declared war on Germany on September 3, 1939. World War II had begun. Hitler's forces conquered Poland in under six weeks, but still, Britain and France did little to halt Hitler's moves or to pressure Germany to retreat.

41

A world at war

Historians usually call the period from September 1939 to April 1940 the "phoney war" because of the inaction of both sides. That soon changed when Germany invaded and conquered Norway in order to secure the Swedish iron imports that came through the country.

Worse was to come. On May 10,

*The map shows the German **blitzkrieg,** or lightning war, that took place 1939–41. **The Nazis new mobile, mechanized tactics defeated one country after another.***

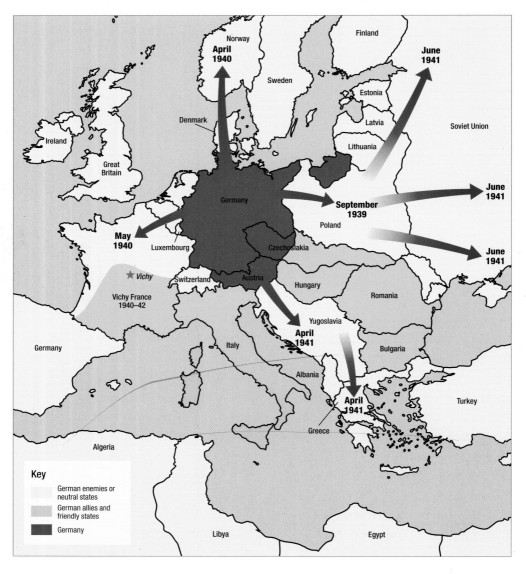

Germany invaded Belgium, the Netherlands, and then France. France was overwhelmed in just six weeks, even though the British army had been sent to help the French. The British narrowly escaped capture when they were rescued from the beaches of Dunkirk and taken back to Britain. Hitler paused, not wishing to gamble on a seaborne invasion of Britain. In September, wave upon wave of German bombers and fighter aircraft attacked Britain, hoping to force her to surrender. Although seriously weakened, Britain held out and the attacks gradually diminished. Hitler transferred his efforts to conquering land in the east to create *lebensraum*, living space carved out of Soviet territory.

On June 22, 1941, Hitler ordered "Operation Barbarossa," the invasion of the Soviet Union. At first, the Germans were victorious, with millions of Soviet prisoners of war falling into their hands, but as the months passed, the weight of huge reserves of Soviet soldiers began to overwhelm the German army.

The world war became global in 1941. In December 1941, the Japanese air force attacked the U.S. Navy at Pearl Harbor. The U.S. joined the war on the side of Britain and the Soviet Union. With the U.S.'s vast resources of men and materials, the defeat of Germany and Japan became inevitable.

The death toll of the Nazi invasion of Eastern Europe was huge. Nazi execution squads in the east shot millions of people, including communist officials and many Jews. Millions of Jews fell into German hands as the conquests spread. Jews were forced into ghettos, and by January 1942, five main concentration camps had been created in a plan to exterminate the entire Jewish race. It is estimated that six million Jews were murdered by the Nazis during

The prisoners of Auschwitz-Birkenau look through the wire following the liberation of the camp by the Allies in 1944.

the Holocaust. One million were shot in the Soviet Union and around four million were gassed or worked to death in the concentration camps. One of the largest and most infamous concentration camps was at Auschwitz-Birkenau in southern Poland. It has been estimated that more than one million people died at Auschwitz.

The end of the Third Reich

The attack on Pearl Harbor was a major turning point in the war for it brought the United States onto the Allied side. No country could match the resources of the U.S. Up until the end of 1941, Germany had known nothing but success. But by the end of 1942, they had been defeated in North Africa and in the Soviet Union at Stalingrad. From then on, the Nazis were in retreat. In June 1944, Allied troops landed in France in a seaborne

In 1945, victorious Soviet soldiers enter Berlin at the end of World War II.

invasion. Germany was forced to fight on two fronts, in the Soviet Union and France. The Germans were gradually pushed back in northern France and

by early 1945, the Allies had crossed the Rhine and entered Germany itself. Soviet soldiers entered Berlin in April.

In the Far East, following the Japanese attack on Pearl Harbor, the U.S. attacked the Japanese-occupied British colonies in Burma and Malaya to gain access to valuable raw materials such as oil. The Battle of Midway in June 1942 was the turning point in the Far East, when the U.S. Navy successfully ambushed the Japanese fleet. The end to the Pacific War came when the U.S. dropped atomic bombs on the Japanese cities of Hiroshima on August 6, 1945 and Nagasaki on August 9. Japan formally surrendered on September 2. Germany and Japan had been decisively beaten and the war was over.

On April 30, 1945, Hitler shot himself in Berlin. Himmler and Goebbels poisoned themselves in May. Hitler had boasted that his regime would survive for 1,000 years; it had lasted for only twelve.

TIMELINE

1933
January — Adolf Hitler is appointed chancellor of Germany.

1934
April — Heinrich Himmler is appointed head of the SS.

June — "Night of the Long Knives" —SA leaders are executed.

1935
Nuremburg anti-Semitic laws are passed.

1936
March — German troops occupy the Rhineland.

August — The Olympic Games are held in Berlin.

Jewish teachers are banned from teaching Aryan children.

1937
Separation of Jews from Aryans at public baths and health resorts.

1938
March — *Anschluss*: all anti-Semitic laws against the Jews in Germany are extended to Austrian Jews.

November — *Kristallnacht*: Jewish property attacked and over 100 Jews murdered.

1939
September — Germany invades Poland marking the beginning of WWII.

1940
April — German troops invade Denmark and Norway.

May — Germany invades the Netherlands, Belgium, and France.

June — France surrenders.

October — The Warsaw ghetto in Poland is constructed.

1941
June — Germany invades the Soviet Union. The *Einsatzgruppen* units begin mass murder of Jewish victims. Murder of the Jews and other victims of the Nazis begins in concentration camps.

December — Germany and Italy declare war on the United States.

1942
July — Deportation of around 300,000 Jews from the Warsaw ghetto to extermination camps begins.

1943
February — The Germans are defeated at Stalingrad.

April — Jewish uprising in the Warsaw ghetto.

October — The Danish underground rescues 7,000 Jews, who escape to Sweden.

1944
June — Allied forces arrive in Normandy in the D-Day landings.

July — Soviet troops liberate the first concentration camp at Majdanek in Poland.

1945
April — Allied troops enter the concentration camps. Hitler commits suicide.

May — Germany surrenders.

November — Nuremberg Trials begin.

1962
May — Adolf Eichmann is executed for war crimes following his trial in Israel in 1961.

GLOSSARY

Allies
Countries at war with Germany and Japan, the "Axis" powers, in WWII.

Annex
The incorporation of a territory into another country or state.

Aryan
Germanic races believed by the Nazis to be the superior race.

Atomic bomb
An explosive device, the power of which is the result of releasing nuclear energy.

Austro-Hungarian Empire
A state in middle Europe consisting of many different ethnic groups. Defeated and broken up into independent states at the end of WWI.

Battle League
A league of patriotic fighting societies and the German National Socialist party in Germany in the 1920s.

Bolshevism
The radical communist group that seized power in the Soviet Union in 1917.

Chancellor
Head of the German government.

Colony
A country that is governed by people living there who represent a foreign government.

Communism
Economic and social system where, in theory, everyone is equal and all property is owned collectively, by the people.

Concentration camp
Prison camp where Jews and others were held in captivity and often worked to death.

Demilitarize
To remove and prohibit the presence of soldiers and weapons.

Einsatzgruppen
Action squads, SS units responsible for the murder of "inferior" racial groups.

Ethnic group
A group of people united by a common religion, race, or culture.

Final Solution
A phrase used by the Nazis to describe their program for the extermination of the Jews.

Fixed pension
A type of pension that is set at a fixed amount.

Freikorps
Bands of extreme right-wing nationalist ex-soldiers formed at the end of WWI.

Ghetto
Area of a town where Jews were forced to live.

Hitler Youth
The Nazis' official youth organization.

Holocaust
The term used after the war to describe the murder of some six million Jews.

Kristallnacht
"Night of Broken Glass." A pogrom against Jews in November 1938.

Lebensraum
Living space. Conquering Eastern Europe for German colonization.

Left-wing
A group in a political organization that is more progressive and radical than others.

Mutiny
A rebellion against authority, usually soldiers or sailors refusing to obey orders.

Nationalist
A person who is passionately loyal to his or her own country.

NSDAP
Nationalsozialistische Deutsche Arbeiterpartei—National Socialist German Worker's Party—the Nazi Party.

Pacific War
War in the Pacific came about after the Japanese attacked the United States at Pearl Harbor in 1941.

Paramilitaries
Civilians who are trained in a military way.

Pogrom
A planned campaign of persecution.

Propaganda
Information or publicity put out by an organization to spread and promote a policy or an idea.

Putsch
A sudden planned attempt to overthrow the government.

Reichstag
The German parliament.

Reparations
The sum of money demanded by the Allies at the end of WWI for war damage.

Right-wing
The more conservative group within a political party or organization.

Russia
The largest country in the world. The last *Tsar,* or king, of Russia was overthrown in 1917. Russia merged with neighboring Soviet republics and became the communist Soviet Union in 1922. Russia became an independent state in 1991 when the Soviet Union collapsed.

SA
Sturm-Abteilung (storm troopers). Nazi paramilitary organization.

Soviet Union
Union of Soviet Socialist Republics (U.S.S.R.), known as Russia, a communist state that existed from 1922 until 1991.

SS
Schutzstaffel—Protection Squad. Nazi elite organization that controlled Nazi Germany.

Third Reich
Name given to the Nazi rule in Germany. *Reich* is the German word for "Empire."

Underground movement
A secret movement that aims to overthrow the government.

Weimar Republic
The name of the republican government in Germany 1919–1933.

FURTHER INFORMATION

FURTHER READING

Nazi Germany by Alex Woolf, Smart Apple Media, 2004

Nazism and War by Richard Bessel, Modern Library, 2006

The Hitler Myth: Image and Reality in the Third Reich by Ian Kershaw, Oxford Univeristy Press USA, 2001

Why Hitler Came into Power by Theodore Abel and Thomas Childers, Harvard University Press, 1986

World War Two by Neil Tonge, Macmillan Children's Books, 2005

Web Sites
Due to the changing nature of Internet links, Rosen Publishing has developed an online list of Web Sites related to the subject of this book. This site is regularly updated. Please use this link to access this list:
http://www.rosenlinks.com/dww/rina

PLACES TO VISIT

United States Holocaust Memorial Museum, 100 Raoul Wallenberg Place, SW Washington, DC 20024-2126

U.S. Air Force Museum, 1100 Spaatz Street, Wright-Patterson Air Force Base, Ohio 45433

U.S.S. Arizona, 1 Arizona Memorial Place, Honolulu, Hawaii 96818
Memorial and museum commemorating the Japanese attack on Pearl Harbor.

INDEX

Numbers in **bold** refer to illustrations.